Stickers!

Page 3

Page 5

Page 7

Page 9

Page 11

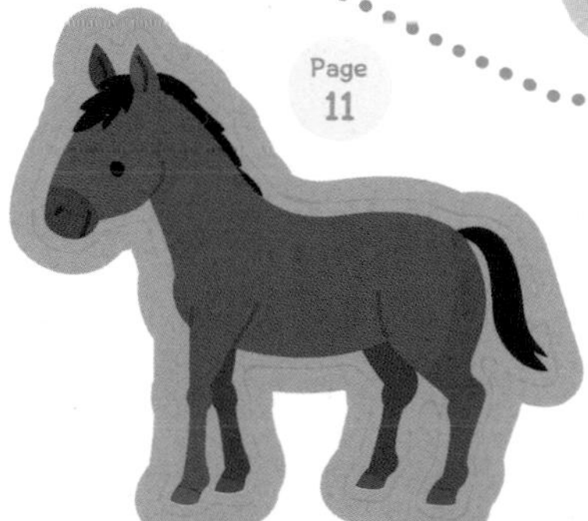

Reward Stickers

Page 13
Page 15
Page 17
Page 19
Page 21
Page 23
Page 25

Page 27

Page 29

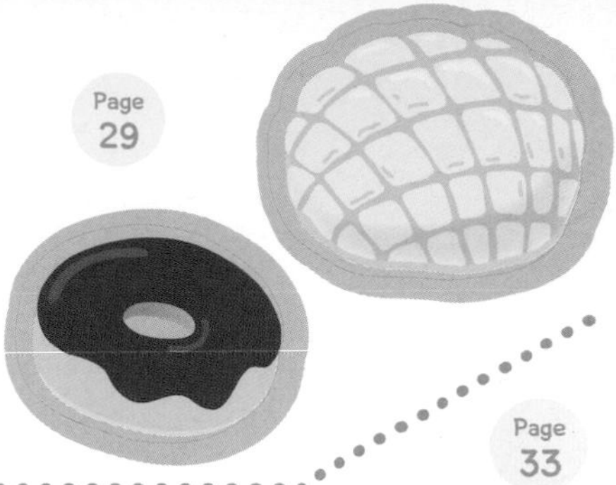

Page 31

Page 33

Page 35

Page 37

Reward Stickers

Page 39
Page 41
Page 43
Page 45
Page 47
Page 49
Page 51

Reward Stickers

Page 61

Page 63

Page 65

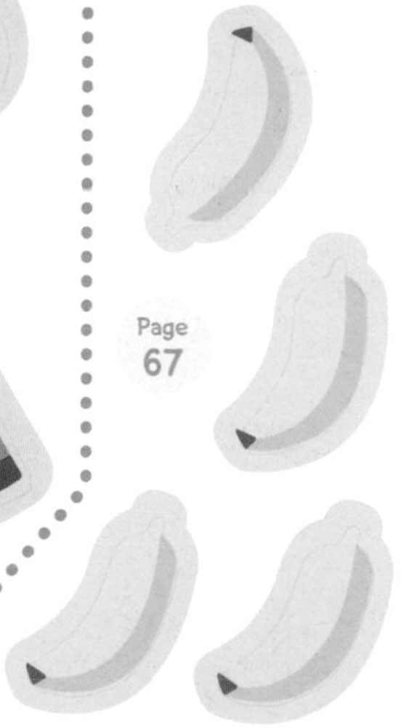

Page 67

Page 69

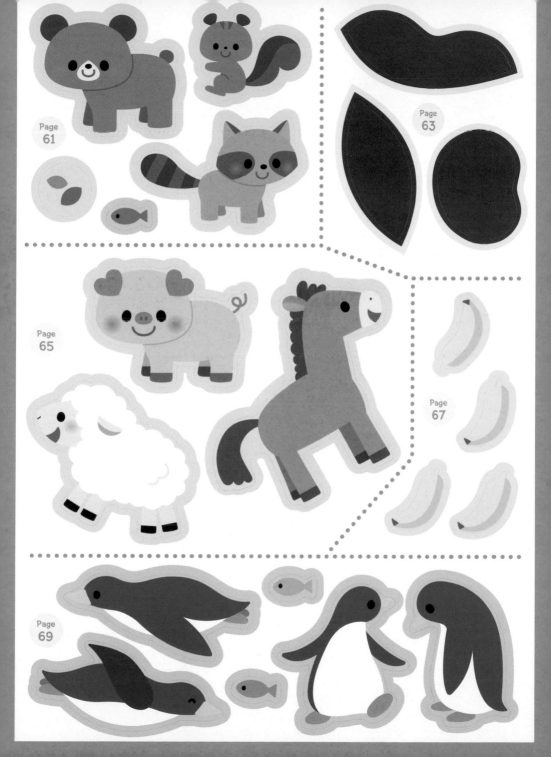

Page 71

Page 73

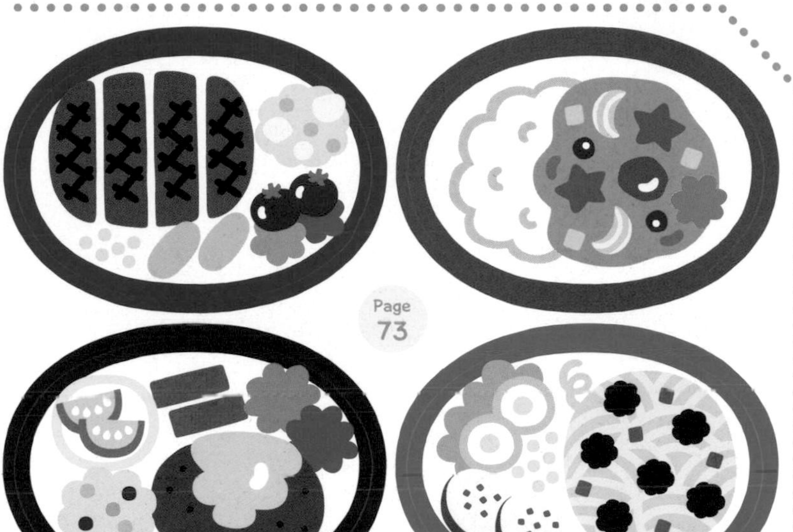

Page 75

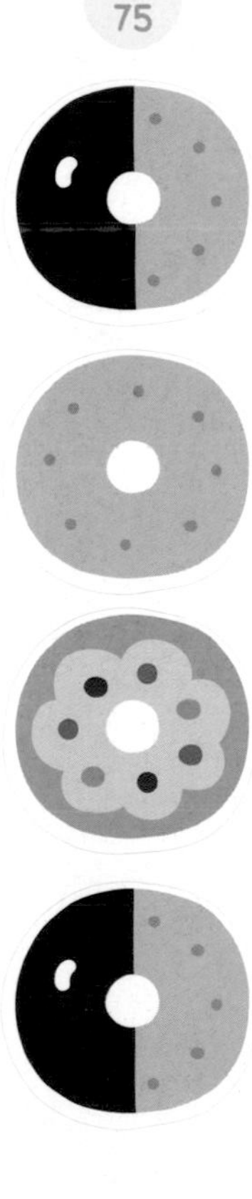

Page 77

Page 79

Reward Stickers

Page 81

Page 83

Page 85

Page 87

Page 89

1 2 3 4

5 6 7 8 9

Page 91

Note to Parents

1) Most of the activities in this book should be at an appropriate developmental level, which will allow your child to do them independently. But don't hesitate to help them! When parents are involved in the learning process, it increases a child's intellectual curiosity and creates a more effective, supportive learning environment.

2) To support your child's learning, review the **"To Parents"** section featured below the instructions. These tips offer parents effective ways to explain the activity to your child.

3) Besides the **sticker activities**, this book includes **additional activities** that use pencils and crayons to develop school readiness skills. By alternating between the sticker pages and the other activities, children will enhance their problem solving skills. These activities include vocabulary enhancement, tracing, find the hidden picture pages, spot the difference games, reasoning, numbers, mazes, drawing, and matching games.

4) When your child finishes the additional activities, let them choose a **reward sticker** to put on the page. Be sure to also praise your child's good work! Be specific with your praise, saying something like, "You did a good job!" or "You were very patient!"

Hold a Crayon

Drawing Lines or Letters

Grip the crayon between your thumb and index finger, and then support it with your middle finger.

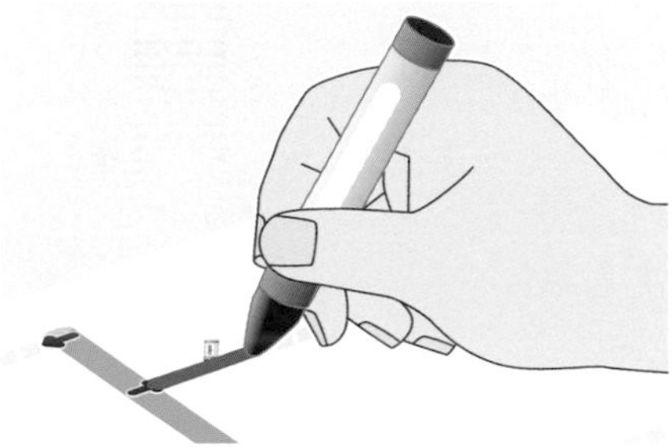

Coloring

Grip the top of the crayon firmly between your thumb and index finger.

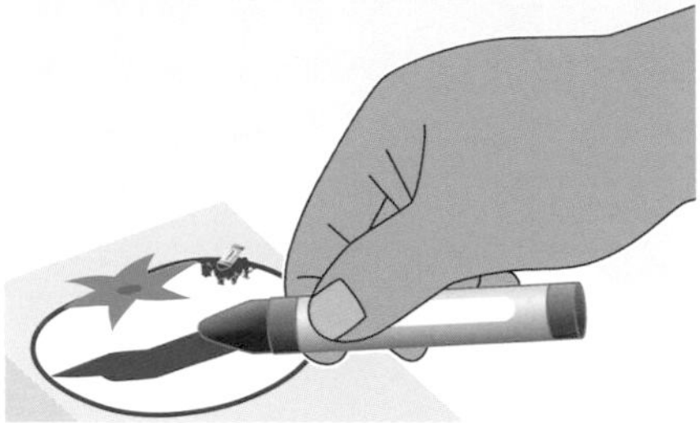

How to Hold a Pencil

Hold the pencil at a 60-degree angle.

Hold the pencil just above the sharpened part. Be careful not to put too much pressure on your fingers.

Grip the pencil between your thumb and index finger, and then support it with your middle finger.

For writing practice, use a shorter, fatter pencil, as it is easier to grip.

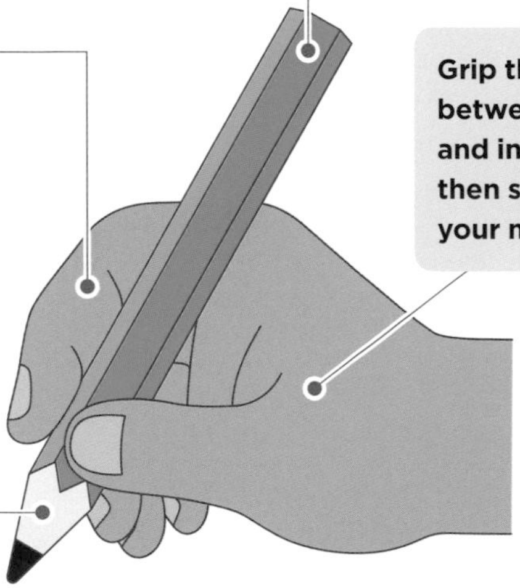

Caution: The paper in this book can be sharp. Take care when handling. This book contains small stickers. Keep out of mouths.

Dog Park

Put the dog sticker on the field.

To Parents | Have your child apply the dog sticker wherever they like.

Name the Animals

Good job!

Point to each animal and say its name.

Rabbit's Playground

Put the rabbit sticker on the floor.
Then give the rabbit a toy.

Draw Lines

Trace lines from ★ to ●.

To Parents | If it seems difficult for your child, put your hand on theirs to help them draw.

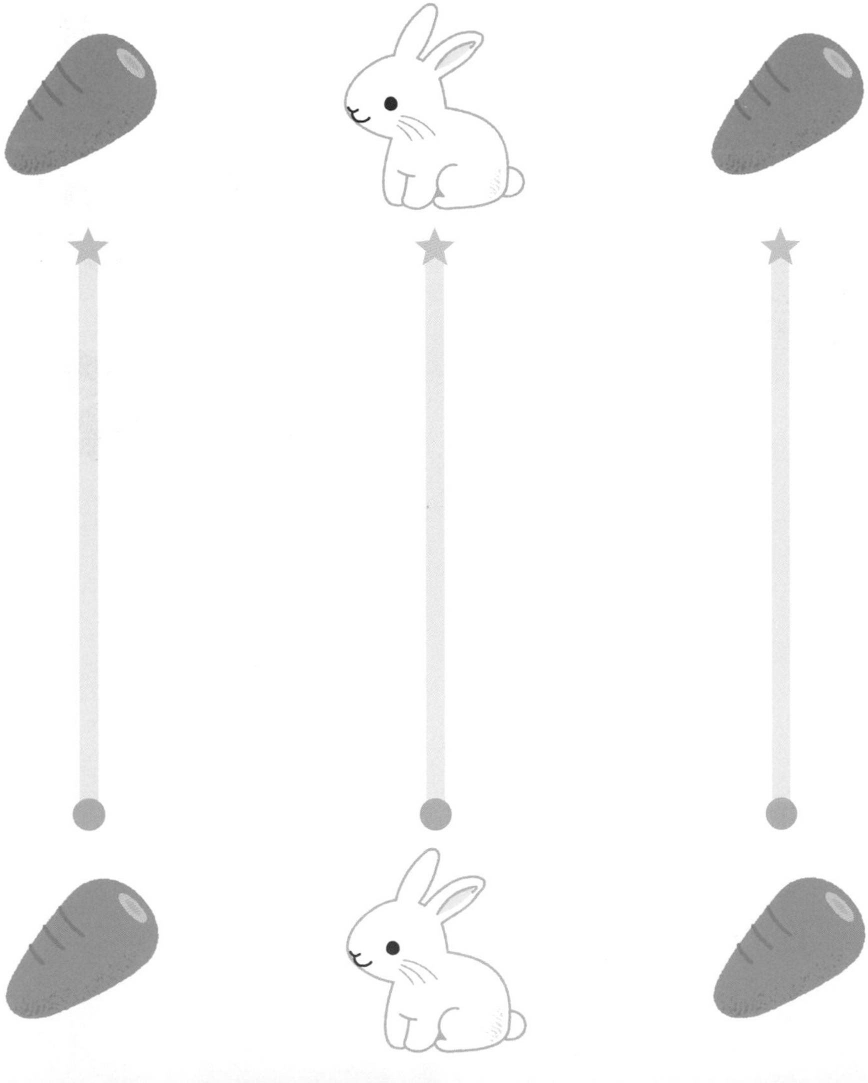

Playful Pandas

Put the panda sticker on the grass.

Find the Same Cat

Good job!

Find the cat that matches the one in the box and point to it.

Find this cat!

Safari Park

Put the animal stickers on the grass.

What's This?

Good job!

Point to each animal and say its name.

Farmyard Fun

Put the animal and the farmer stickers on the page.

Draw Lines

Good job!

Trace lines from ★ to ●.

To Parents | Have your child use a crayon, marker, or pencil depending on your child's ability

Sea Animals

Put the animal stickers in the sea.

Spot the Difference

Find one difference between the top and bottom pictures.

Good job!

To Parents | First count the number of orange fish and blue fish in both pictures together.

Happy Hamster

Put the hamster sticker on the child's palms.

Find Pairs

Good job!

Draw a line from ● to ● to match each animal with its baby.

Frogs in the Pond

Put the frog sticker on the lily pad. Then add some raindrops.

Which Is More?

Good job!

Color the ○ next to the larger number of crabs.

○

○

Tiger Stripes

Put the sticker on the ▇ to complete the tiger's stripes.

Find the Same Wolf

Find the animal that matches the one in the box and point to it.

Find this wolf!

Forest Animals

Put the animal stickers on the matching shadows.

Draw Lines

Good job!

Trace lines from ★ to ●.

To Parents | Encourage your child to pause at each bend before changing direction.

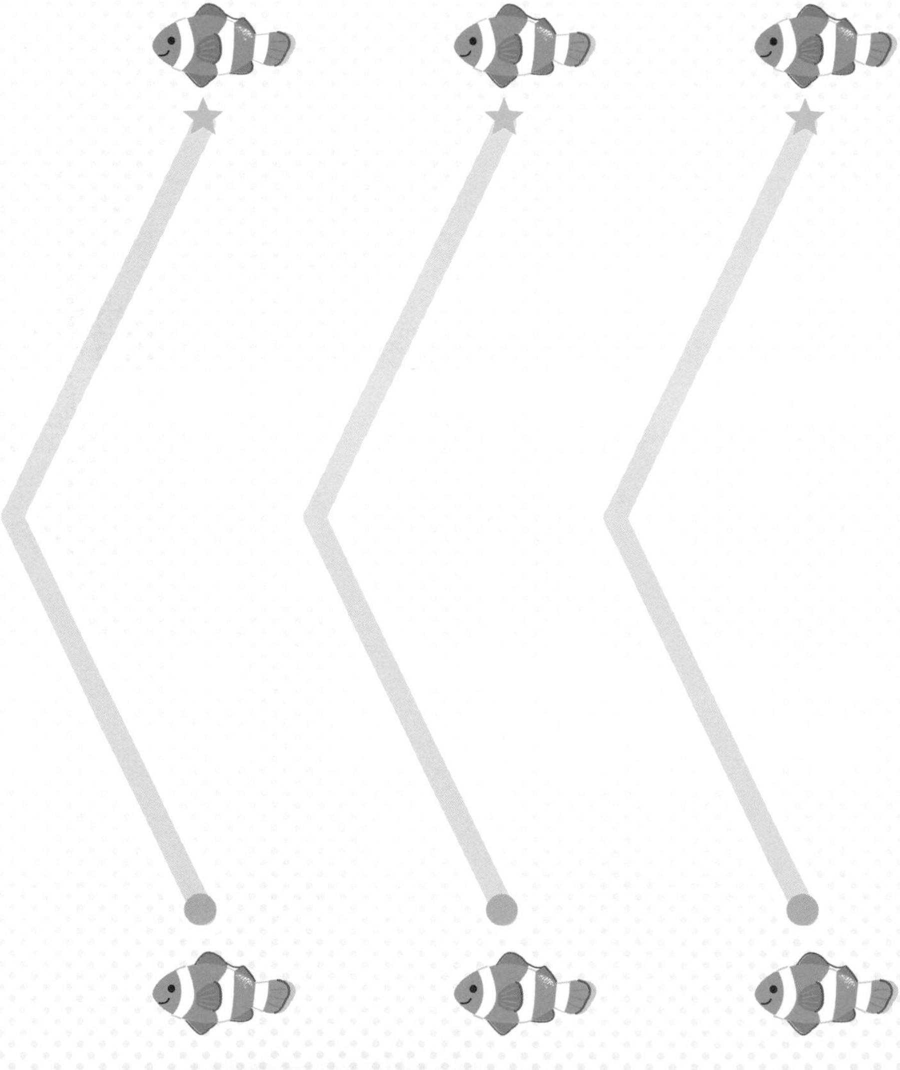

Polar Animals

Put the animal stickers on the matching shadows.

Which Is More?

Color the ◯ next to the larger number of monkeys.

To Parents | Ask your child to draw a line from a monkey at the top to one at the bottom, one by one. The set with the extra monkey has more.

◯

◯

Finish the Pig's Face

Put the nose sticker on the pig.

Spot the Difference

Good job!

Find one difference between the top and bottom pictures.

To Parents | Ask your child what the child is doing in each picture.

Top

Bottom

Flower Shop

Put the flower pot stickers in the shop.

Find the Same Sunflower

Good
job!

Find the flower that matches the one in the box and point to it.

Find this flower!

Fresh Pastries

Put the pastry stickers on the tray.

To Parents While shopping, start a conversation with your child. This is a good opportunity to build vocabulary.

Find the Bakery

Good job!

Find the bakery, and point to it.

To Parents | Ask your child what each store is selling.

Candy Shop

Put the candy and cookie jar stickers on the shelves.

What's This?

Good job!

Point to each dessert and say its name.

cake

ice cream cone

donut

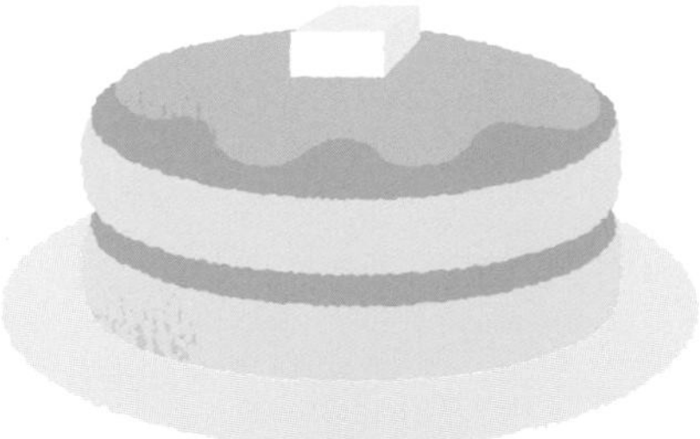

pancakes

Birthday Cake

Decorate the cake with the strawberry stickers.

Find the Baker

Find and point to the baker. Can you name the store where the baker's cake might be sold?

Hamburger Diner

Put the stickers on the tray to make a meal.

Draw Lines

Good job!

Trace lines from ★ to ●.

To Parents | This activity practices drawing circles clockwise and counter clockwise. Before drawing, have your child trace each circle with their finger.

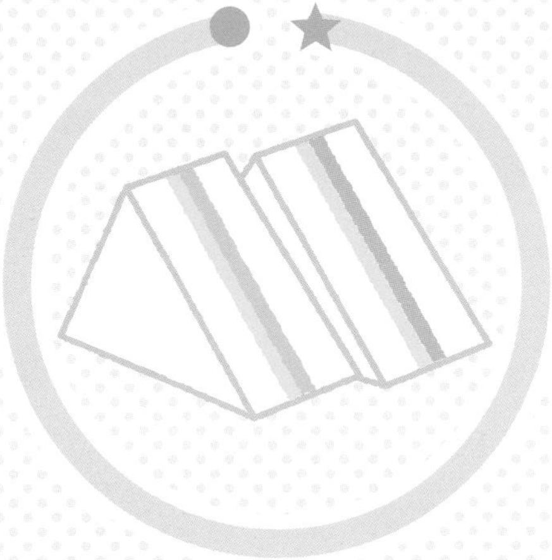

Toy Shop

Put the toy stickers on the shelves.

What's This?

Point to each "set of objects" and say their name.

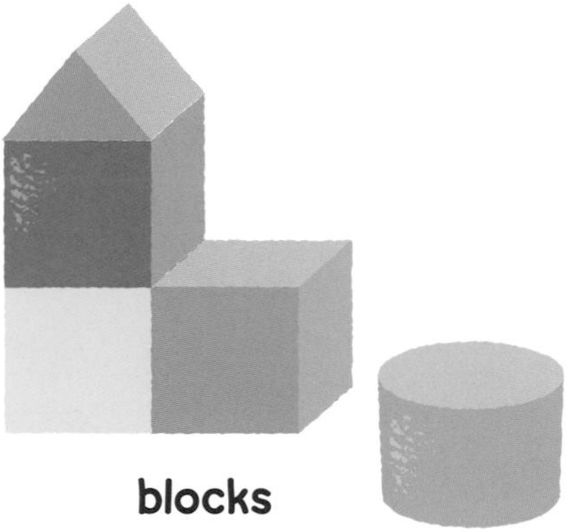

blocks

balloons

crayons

picture books

Pizza Time

Put the stickers on the matching shadows.

Spot the Difference

Good job!

Find one difference between the top and bottom pictures.

Coffee Shop

Put the clock sticker on the wall, the coffee cup sticker on the counter, and the apron sticker on the server.

Draw Lines

Trace lines from ★ to ●.

To Parents | This activity focuses on drawing jagged lines. Encourage your child to pause at each bend before changing direction.

Grocery Store

Put the fruit stickers on the matching shadows.

Colors

Find all the red fruits and point to them.

strawberry

grapes

pineapple

orange

cherries

apple

bananas

Clothing Shop

Put the clothes stickers on the hangers.

Which Is More?

Color the ◯ next to the larger number of balloons.

To Parents Draw a line from a balloon at the top to one at the bottom, one by one. The set with the extra balloon has more.

Share Chocolates

Put two chocolate stickers on each plate.

What's This?

Point to each body part and say its name.

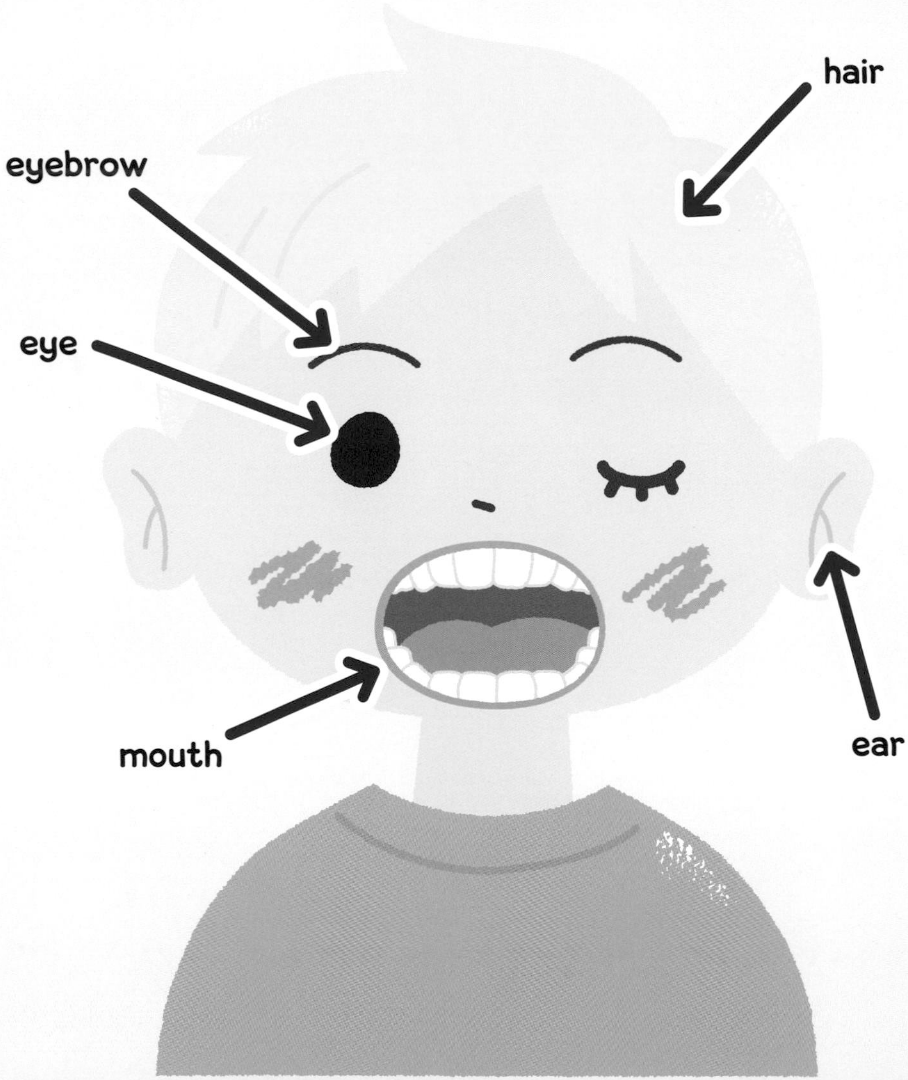

Clothes Pattern

Put the stickers on the boy's clothes to match the picture in the box.

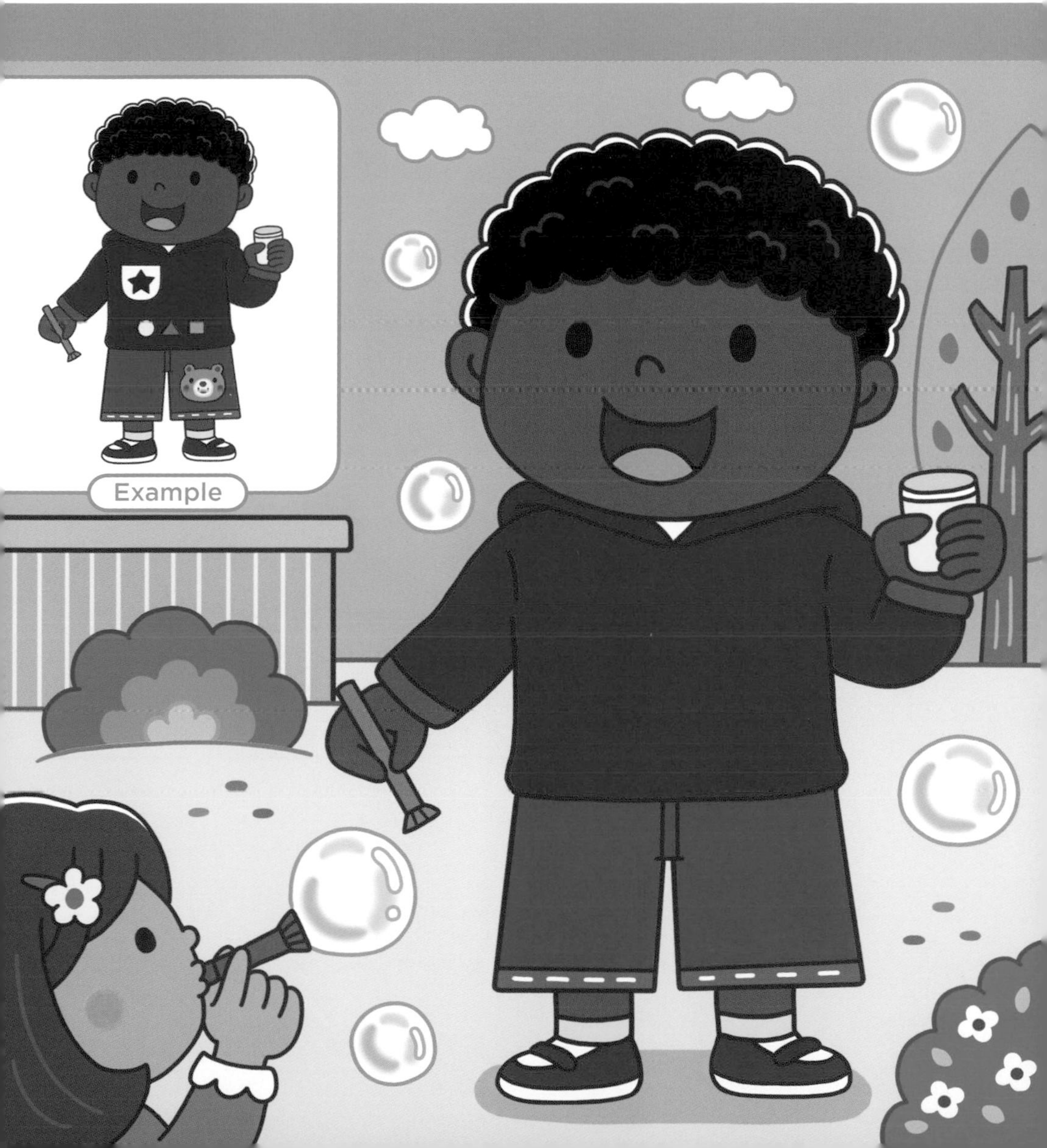

What's This?

Point to each object and say its name.

To Parents | Ask your child what each object is used for.

hat

eyeglasses

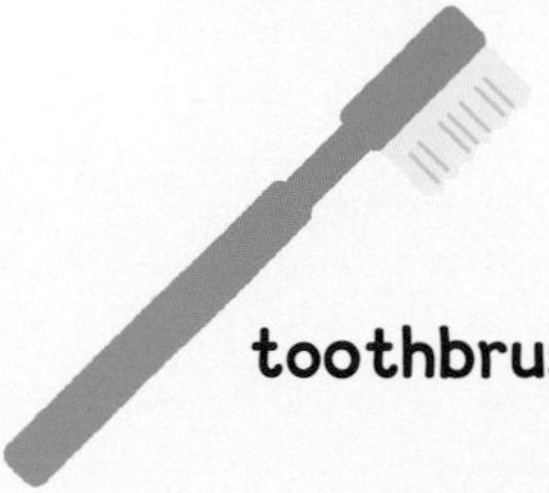

toothbrush

scissors

slide

mailbox

Playful Puppies

Put the puppy stickers on the field.
Then add the other stickers.

Find the Same Dog

Find the dog that matches the one in the box and point to it.

To Parents | First ask your child to find the dogs whose ears match the ones on the dog in the box. Next, have your child find the dogs with the same collar, and then find the dogs with the same pattern.

Cozy Kittens

Put the kitten stickers in the room. Then give them another mouse toy.

To Parents Encourage your child to put stickers on the empty space freely. This activity leads to developing fine motor skills and enriching the imagination.

Find the Same Cat

Find the cat that matches the one in the box and point to it.

To Parents | Have your child pay attention to the color of the cat's fur, collar, and tail pattern.

Zoo Animals

Put the animal stickers on the matching shadows.

Spot the Difference

Find the animals that switched places in the top and bottom pictures.

Top

Bottom

Panda Pals

Put the panda stickers on the field.

Find the Baby Panda

Find the baby panda and circle it.

To Parents | Giant pandas are pink and hairless when they are born. Look up a picture of a baby panda and show it to your child.

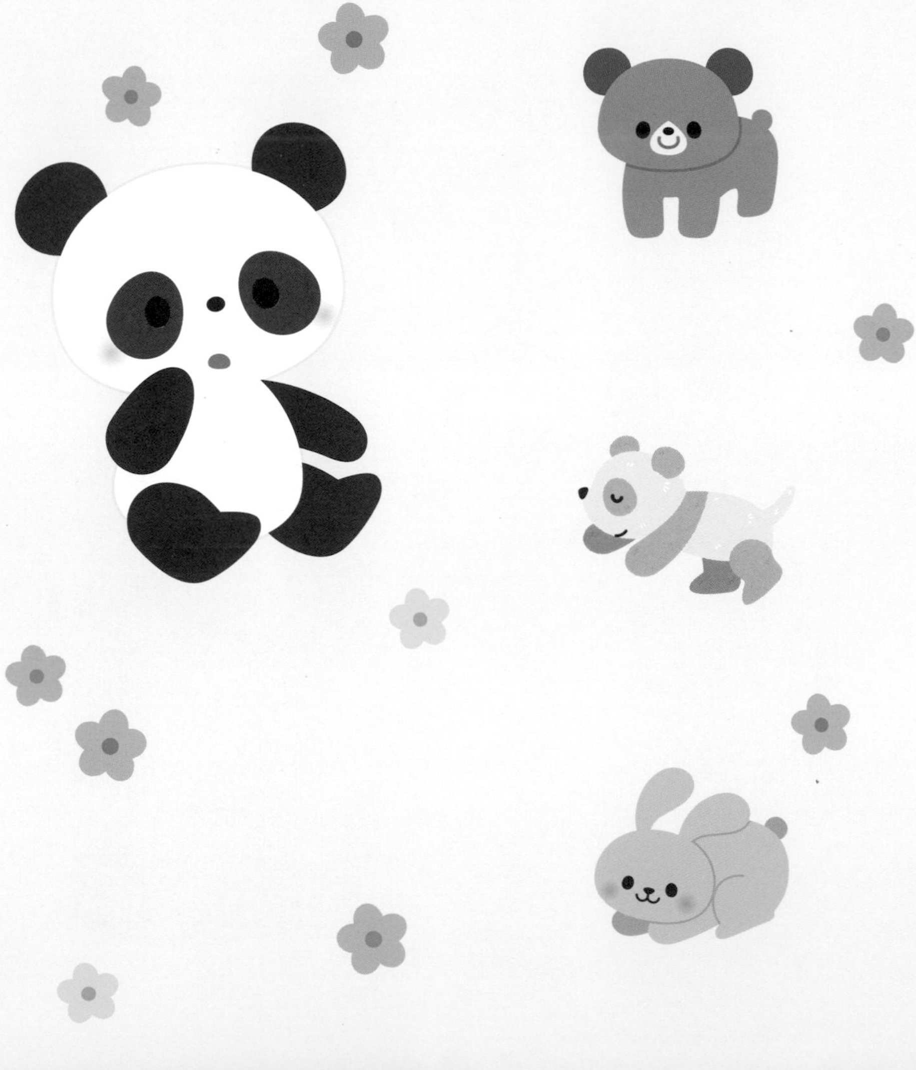

Mommy and Me

Put each baby animal sticker with its mom.

Find Pairs

Draw a line from ● to ● to match each animal with its baby.

Forest Animals

Put the animal stickers on the matching shadows. Then add the other stickers to the page.

Play Hide-and-Seek

Good job!

The animals on the previous page are playing hide-and-seek. Find all five animals.

To Parents | Work on this page after completing page 61.

Cow Colors

Put the stickers on the cow to make a pattern.

Animal Patterns

Draw a line from ● to ● to match the animal to its pattern.

Animal Friends

Put the animal stickers on the matching shadows.

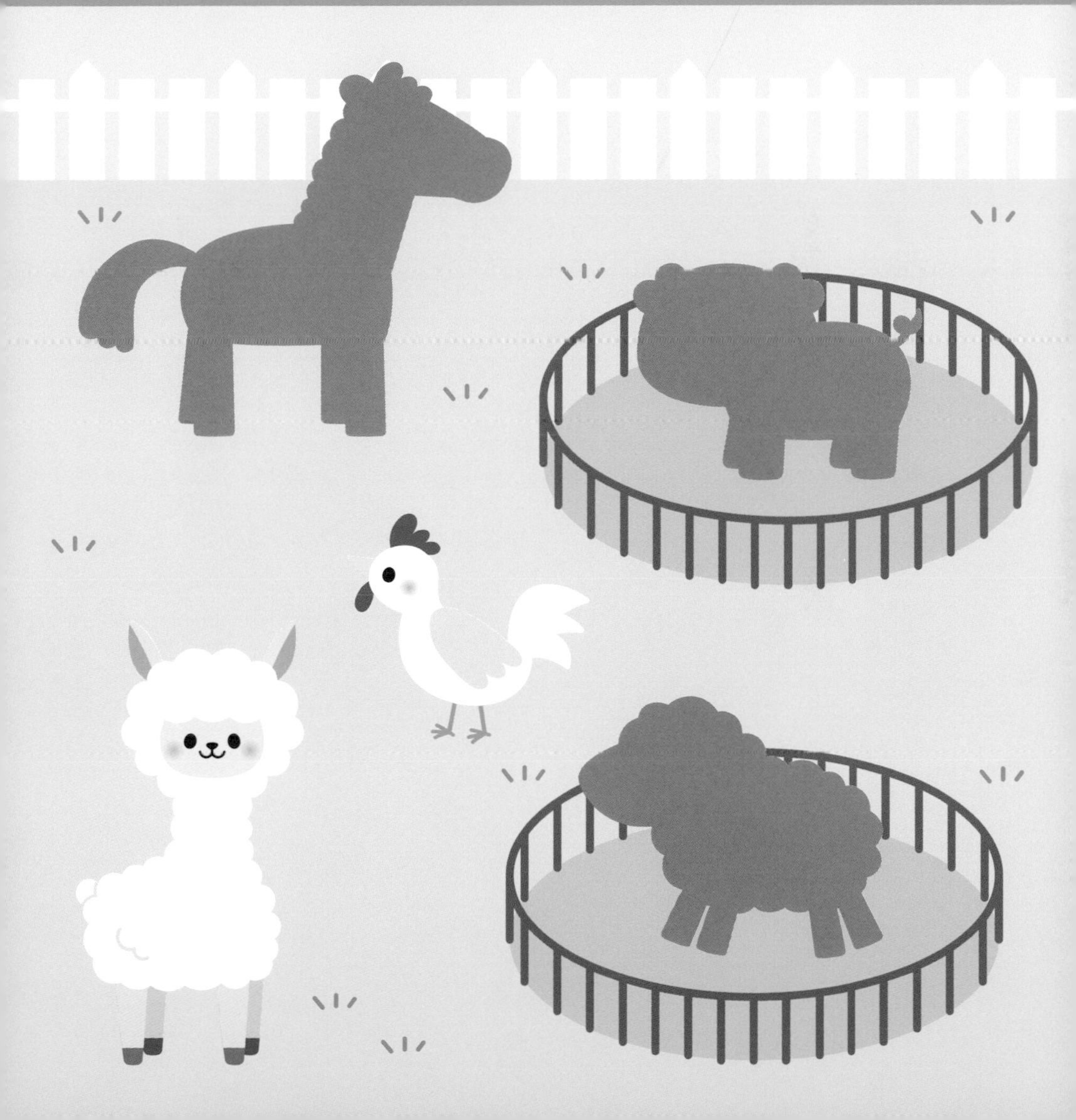

Animal Walk

Draw a line from ● to ● to match the animal to its feet.

Banana Bunch

Use the stickers to give each monkey a banana.

Who Is Missing?

Find the monkey in the top picture that is missing in the bottom picture.

To Parents | First draw a line from a monkey at the top to the matching one at the bottom. Then ask your child which monkey is missing at the bottom.

Top

Bottom

Lively Penguins

Put the penguin stickers on the picture.
Then add the fish stickers to the water.

What's This?

Say the name of each sea animal.

dolphin

octopus

crab

squid

seal

turtle

Tasty Treat

Put the ice cream topping stickers on the sundae.

Find the Same Sundae

Find the ice cream sundae that matches the one in the box and point to it.

To Parents | Make sure to point out the sundae ingredients: a strawberry at the top, strawberries along the brim of the cup, and strawberries inside the cup.

Lunchtime

Put a lunch plate sticker in front of each student.

Find the Same Plate

Good job!

Find the plate that matches the one in the box and point to it.

To Parents Make sure to point out the items on the plate: french fries, tomatoes, and fried chicken.

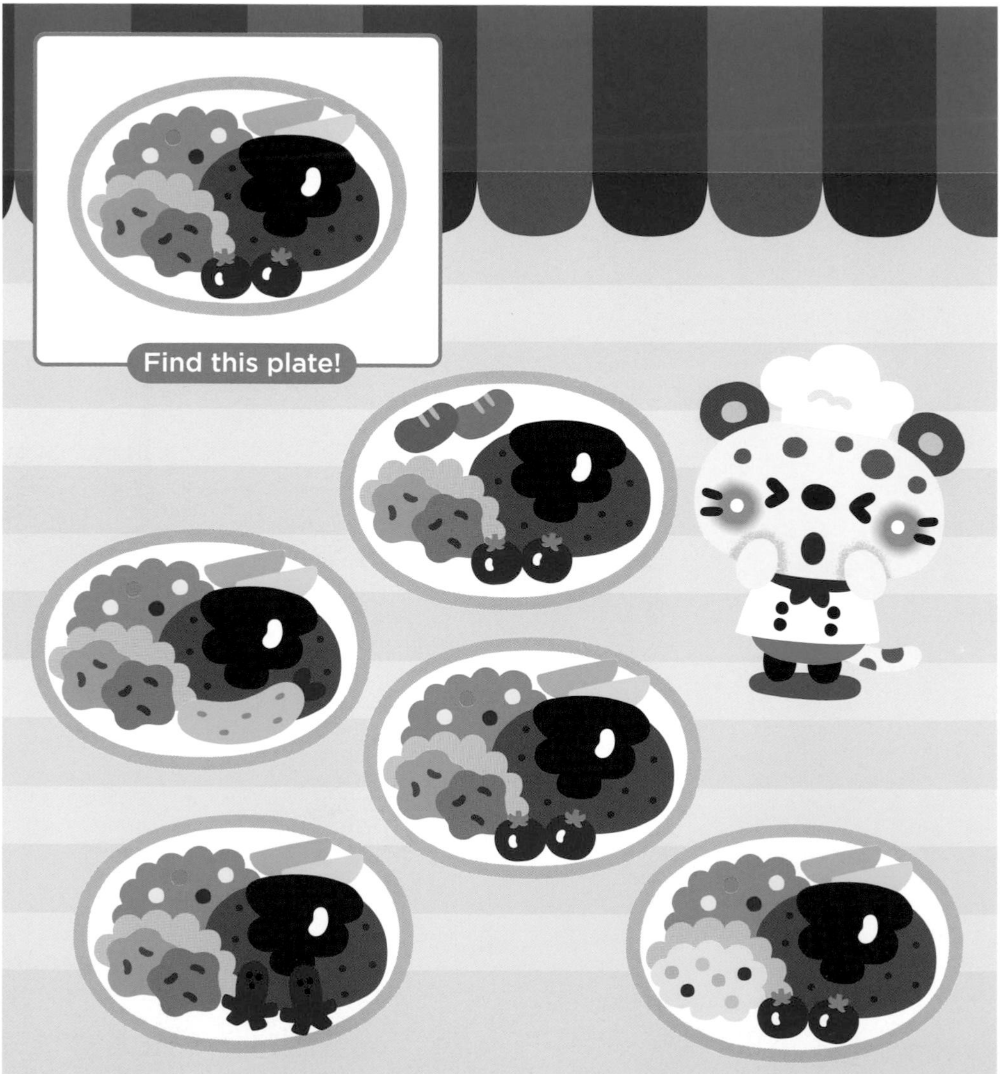

Donut Shop

Put the donut stickers in each box so they have the same donuts as the top box.

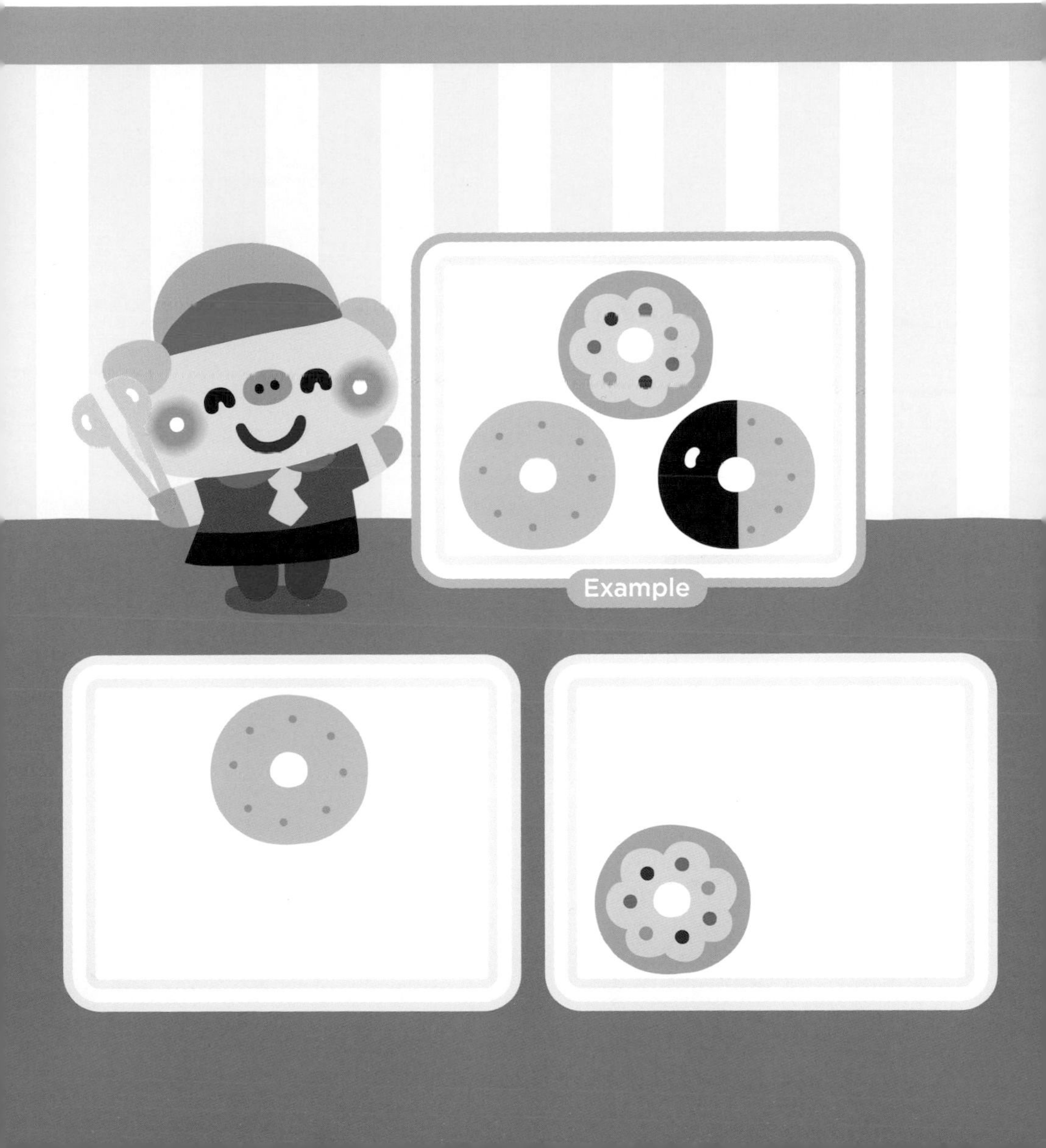

Donut Match

Find a pair of matching donut combinations.

To Parents This activity might seem difficult. Check the boxes one by one. Answer: The top right box matches the bottom middle box.

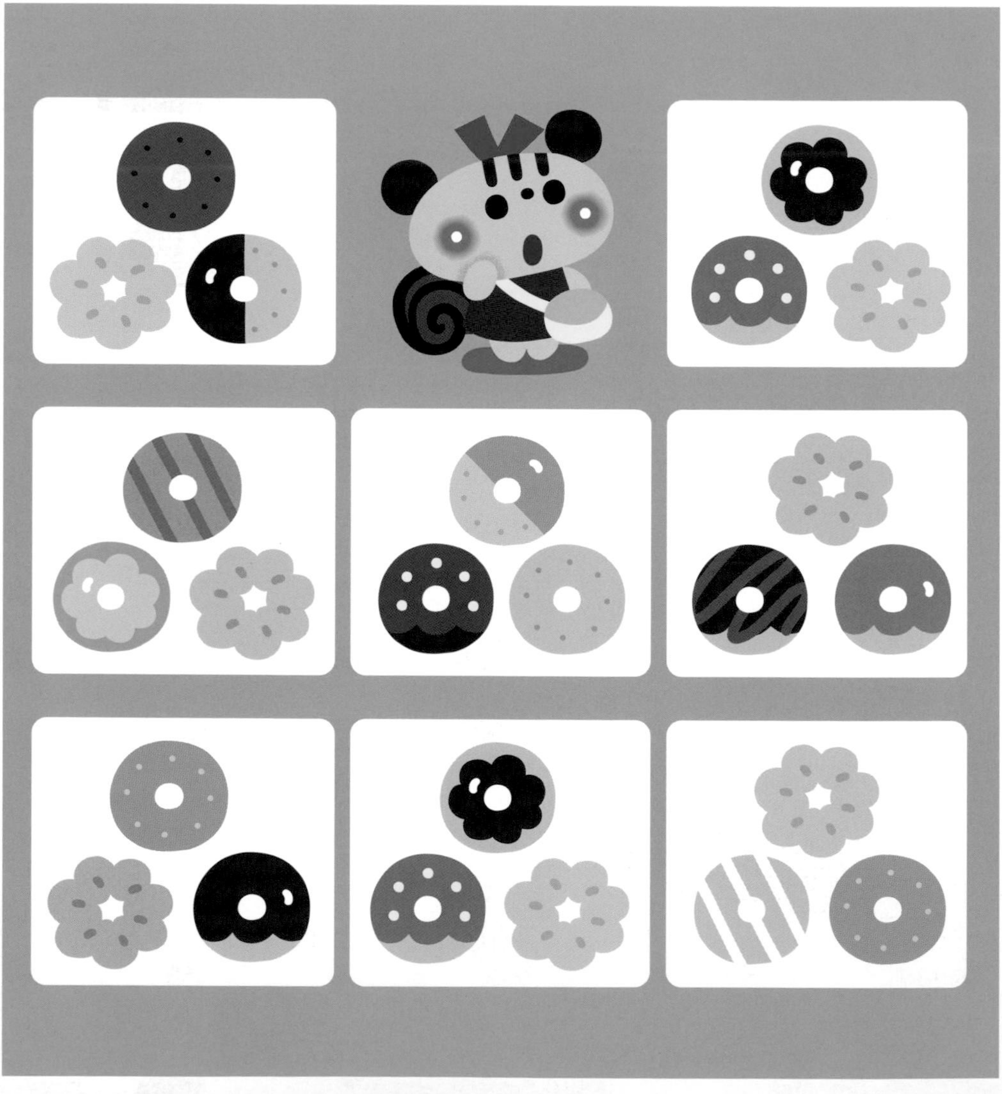

Cheeseburger Meals

Put the stickers on the matching shadows.

Match Numbers

Good job!

Draw lines from ● to ● to match the number of mugs to the number of mice.

To Parents | Encourage your child to draw lines connecting the pairs between the left and right pictures. If needed, help them count from three to five.

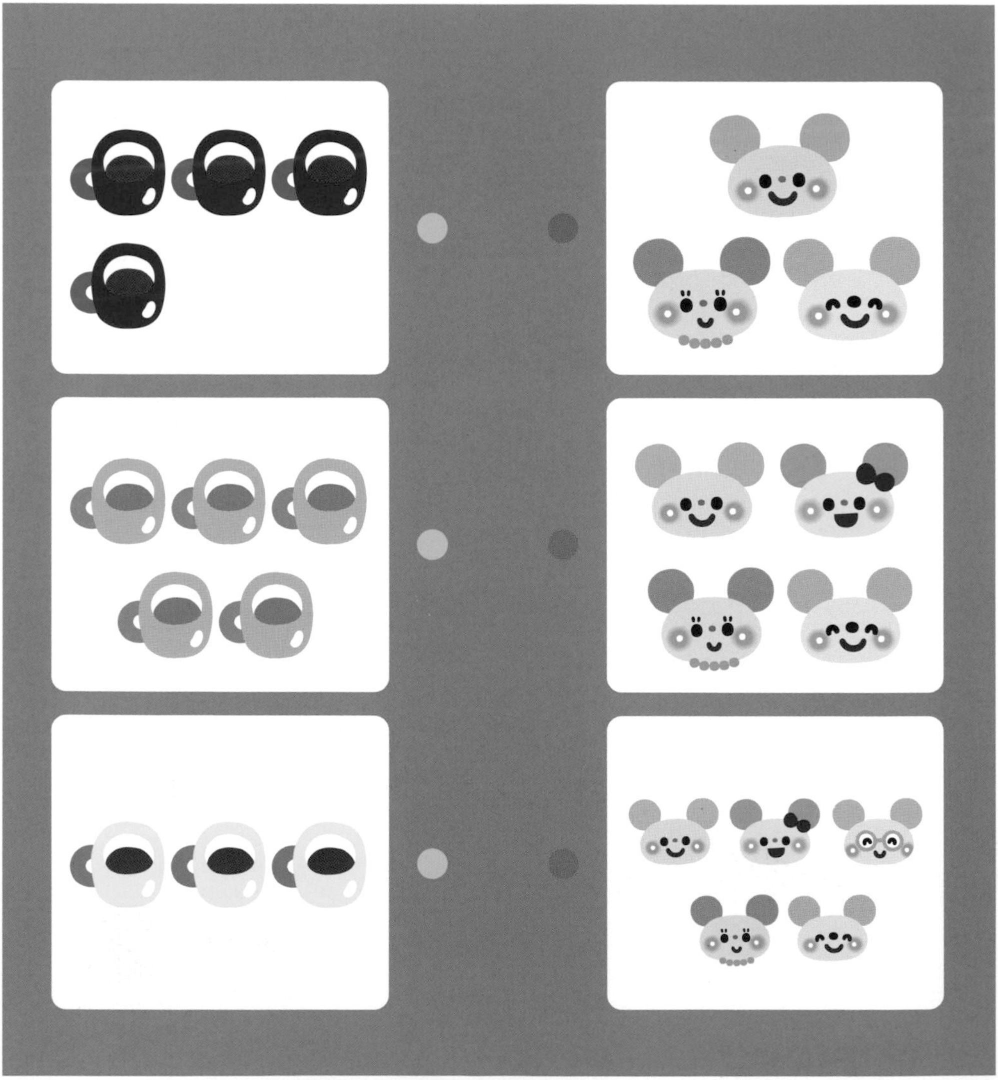

Vegetable Section

Put the vegetable stickers on the matching shadows.

Vegetable Names

Good job!

Say the name of each vegetable.

To Parents | If your child doesn't recognize a vegetable, point it out while food shopping to reinforce the vocabulary word.

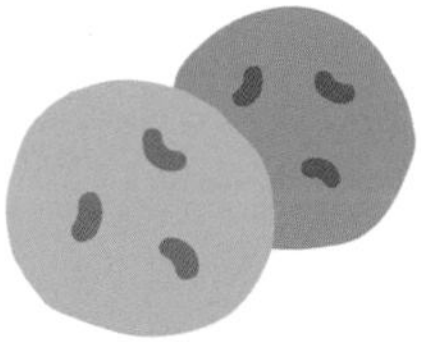

potatoes

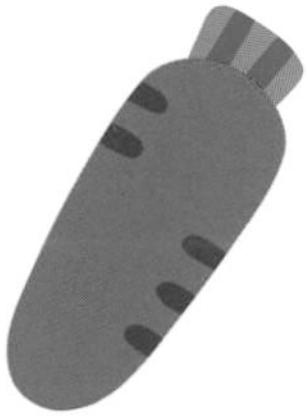

carrot

peas

radish

eggplant

lettuce

onion

spinach

Food Shopping

Put the fruit stickers on the matching shadows.

Find the Different Plate

Find the plate that does not have the same fruits as the one in the box and point to it.

To Parents | Encourage your child to look at the items in the box by saying, "Orange, apple, and grapes."

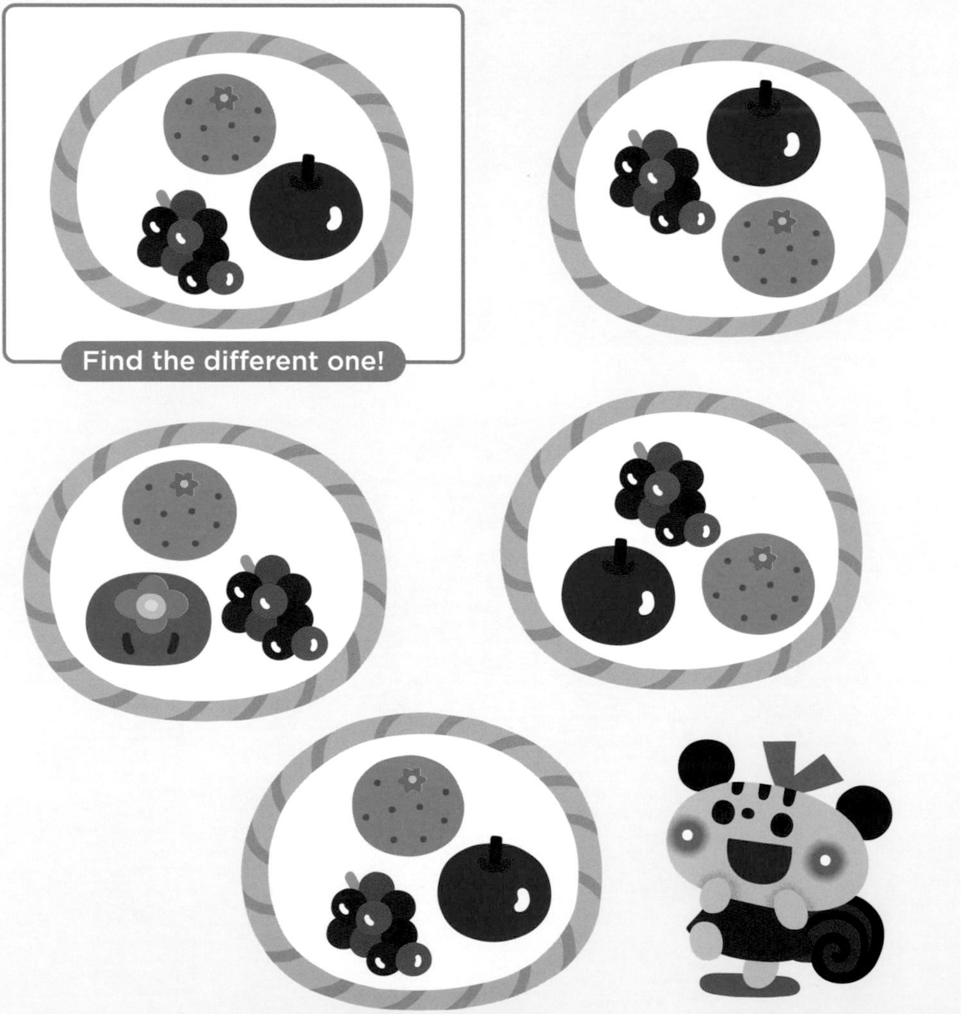

Level 2 ★★☆

Toy Shop

Put the toy stickers on the shelves.

To Parents Encourage your child to put the toy stickers on the page. There are four shelves and five stickers. Your child can decide where each sticker should go.

Playground Path

Follow the path from ➡ to ➡ and pick up all the tools to play with in the sandbox.

To Parents Tell your child simple rules, such as "Go from the start to the finish" or "Do not pass the same way twice."

Bookstore

Put the book stickers on the matching ▇ to finish the covers.

Hidden Picture

Find three  in the bookstore.

Find the Store

Put each sticker in the store where it is sold.

Matching Groups

Draw lines from ● to ● to match things that go together.

Number Match

Count the objects in each box.
Then place the matching number sticker in the ▇.

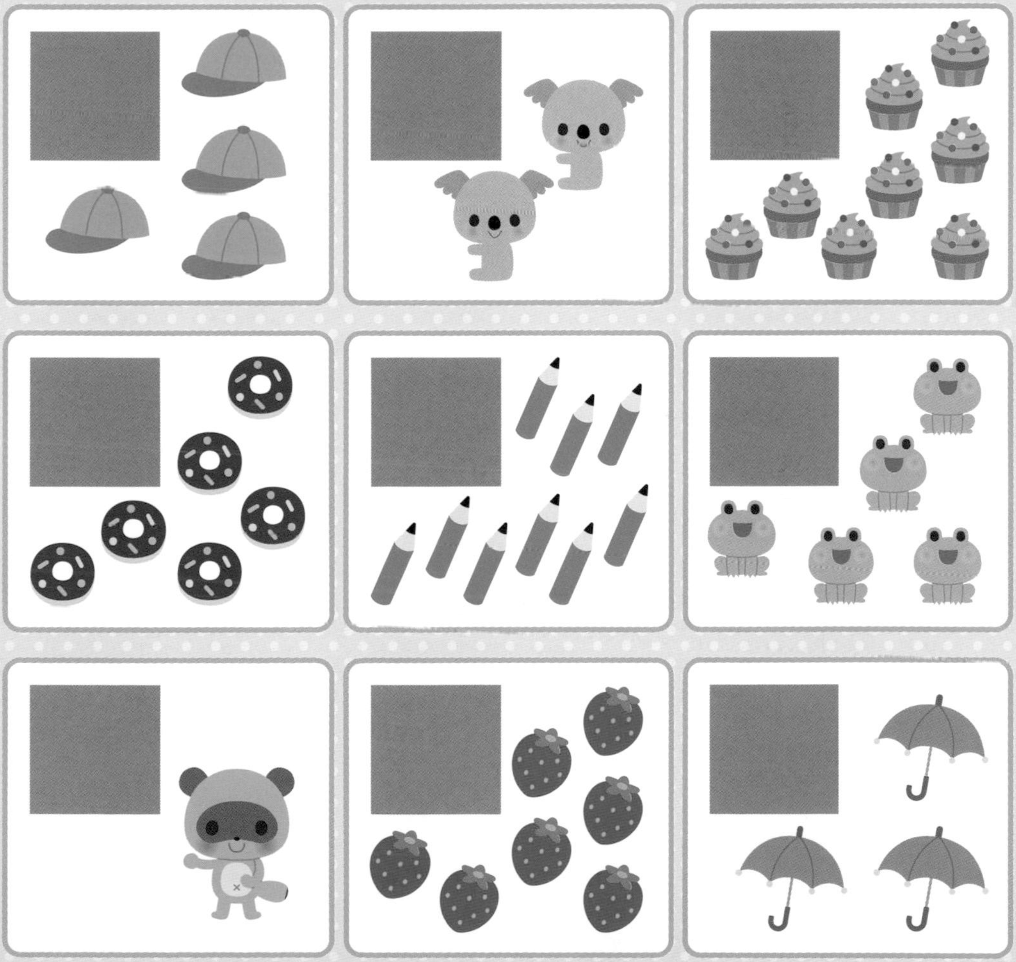

Numbers and Pictures

Good job!

Draw lines from ● to ● to match the numbers and pictures.

To Parents | Have your child point to each object as they count. If your child has difficulty recognizing the numbers, write down the number your child counted.

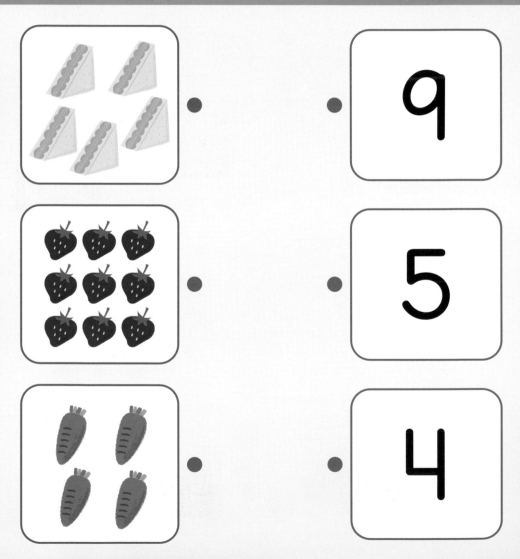

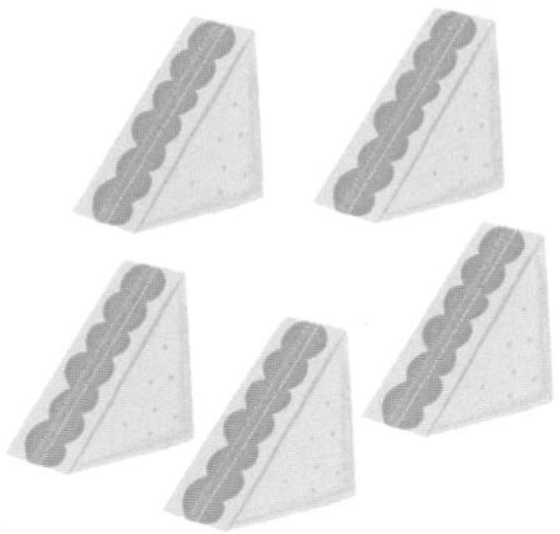

9

5

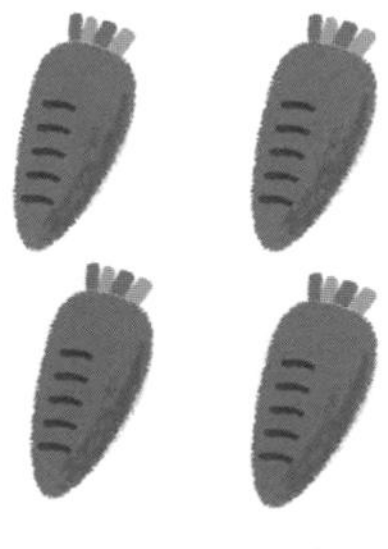

4

Go Fishing

Trace each line and put the matching fish sticker in the tank.

Find the Flower Shop

Good job!

Find the flower shop and point to it.

Find the Same Treat

Good job!

Find the ice cream treat that matches the one in the box and point to it.

Save the Seals!

Good job!

Trap the shark by drawing lines from ● to ●.

Find the Same Ice Cream Cone

Good job!

Find the ice cream cone that matches the one in the box and point to it.

To Parents | Draw a line from each ice cream scoop in the box to the matching ice cream scoop.

Find this ice cream cone!

Which Is More?

Good job!

Color the ○ next to the larger number of acorns, birds, and fish.

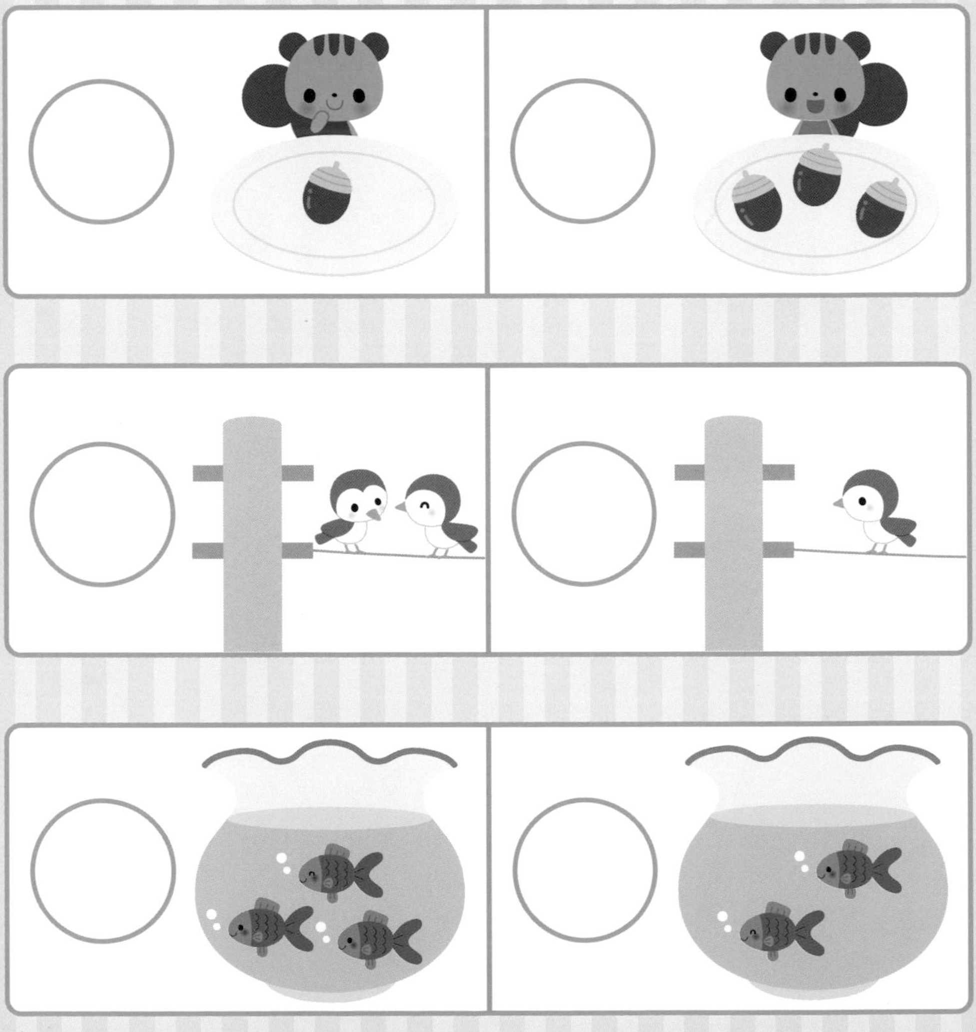